Jordan's Near Side

Frank Stafford Davis

Jordan's Near Side

by Frank Stafford Davis

Jordan's Near Side
　　by Frank Stafford Davis

Photographs by:
　　Peter Martin and Frank Stafford Davis, all rights re-
served by each photographer (photo credits on page 97).

Edited and layout by:
　　Charles Morello
　　IRIS Enterprises
　　Eveleth, MN 55734

Published by:
　　Singing River Publications, Inc.
　　P.O. Box 72
　　Ely, MN 55731
　　www.speravi.com/singingriver
　　SAN: 254 - 136X

Printed by:
　　service printers of duluth, inc.
　　127 East Second Street
　　Duluth, MN 55805

ISBN:
　　0-9709575-7-2

1. Rural Culture; 2. Pastoral Reminiscences; 3. Midwest Region; 4. Northeast Region; 5. Spiritual Life; 6. Americana;
7. Creation Spirituality

DEDICATION

This book is dedicated to Robert Thayer Sataloff, M.D., of Philadelphia, Pennsylvania. Through the grace of God, Dr. Sataloff used his extraordinary abilities as a surgeon and a healer to restore my voice when I thought all was lost. I am forever grateful to him.

INTRODUCTION AND ACKNOWLEDGEMENTS

From as far back as I can remember, I always felt a certain emptiness in the ways that church-going people talked about their beliefs. Growing up, it was my experience that most preachers, Sunday School teachers, and other well-intentioned Christians seemed to say that our spiritual lives are about something higher, better, truer and ultimately beyond the eve-ryday world of people, places and events. I knew that there was something important, perhaps even partially true, about these words of my elders. But to my young heart, it appeared that these teachers wanted to disconnect the realm of God from the ordinary world – which they seemed to view as drab and uninteresting. For these good Christians, this life was just something to get through, so you could get to the Promised Land on the River Jordan's far shore and to your final reward of being with God and all your relatives who had passed away in previous years. They called it eternal life and it didn't sound too bad. But, the part that never made sense to me was their assessment of this world; this life as being essentially dull, gray and sorrow-filled. From an early age, the near side of the Jor-dan always looked pretty good to me, if not extraordinary.

The world outside the window of my childhood was, from the beginning, filled with mystery and the scent of the Creator. The world I began to know was rich, colorful, joyful, difficult and sometimes dangerous. There were challenges, victories and disappointments. But most of all there was the sense that the world in which I lived was enchanted in a deep, abiding man-ner. The Georgia woods I explored as a young boy were alive. There were huge poplars that inspired imagination and creek bottoms that made the hair stand up on the back of your neck. In the summer, furious and magnificent thunderstorms roared across the deep green landscape with the message that all creation is connected. God is in everything and everyone. Likewise, from the start, there were the people – the characters who were the bearers of God's mystery – sometimes perfectly cast, and at other times redolent in irony but no less revelatory of that "something more" that I have come to understand as the Divine. There were the rural politicians with deep, sweet drawls and strong opinions about everything from the University of Georgia football team to how best to manage the vast pinelands of the southeast part of the state. There were Black fishing guides in north Florida, who told stories all day long while taking us to all the best fishing spots. Their dark eyes and melodious voices brought the mystery of Africa into a ten-year-old's mind and heart. North Georgia brought the mountain 'prophet' Buford into my life. His "nectars of the wild" were always worth the price you paid. His wisdom was for free. These experiences with places and people taught me that I could find God anywhere, anytime if . . . I opened my eyes and heart. This approach has stayed with me. If anything, it has gotten deeper.

I have lived on Minnesota's Mesabi Iron Range since 1988. I have found it to be a remarkable place. It is for me a magical realm of the far north. If you take the time to get beneath the taconite dust, you uncover the treasure of people who still speak with the accents of their home countries. The quaking leaves of the aspens murmur the spirit voices of the Ojibwe who lived in harmony with this land for so many years. In many respects people on the Range live closer to the earth and sky than their urban, suburban and exurban cousins. They plant vegetable gardens in tiny backyard plots and cut and split many cords of wood to keep their homes warm during the long winter months. Brush away the taconite dust, and you find yourself in a pretty extraordinary place, wondering why anyone would ever think of the Range as the least bit ordinary.

In the stories and photographs collected in this volume, it is my intent to share with the reader my certainty that God is in and around us at all times and in all places. The Divine can be readily found in the ordinary circumstances of our lives – if we are willing to set aside some of the ecclesiastical, theological and cultural blinders which prevent us from seeing the world freshly. Even in our darkest moments, we can, if we choose to, find sure evidence of God's presence and, thereby, discover the hope to continue traveling the enchanted terrain of our lives.

I wish to acknowledge, with deep gratitude, a number of people and groups who knowingly and sometimes unknowingly played a part in helping me put this book together.

My wife, Kristin Foster, my shadow, who urged me to write as a way of expressing a God-given ability. Her support of my writing has been strong and unwavering.

My daughters, Tyler and Emily, whose lives bring me deep joy in the core of my heart.

Anita Kozan, Ph. D., who supported me with her profound knowledge and understanding of voice, and her deep abiding spirit of compassion.

Mary St. Michael, a true healer, who set me firmly on the path of knowing and speaking my own truth.

The congregations I have served since I was ordained in Pittsburgh, Pennsylvania in 1982. In these communities of nurture and love I have learned so much about God and human beings.
-Hoboken Presbyterian Church, Blawnox, PA
-St. James Presbyterian Church, Tower, MN
-Hope Community Presbyterian Church, Virginia, MN

John Rockwell, a fellow pilgrim from early days whose presence remains in my life as a source of wisdom

The family in which I grew up. My parents Ovid and Ruby Davis, who did not live to see the publication of this book, but who always encouraged me to write. And my brother

Brant Davis, who remains a loving witness to those earliest people, places and events that helped us become who we are today.

Christine Moroni of *Singing River Publications* and Chuck Morello of *IRIS Enterprises*. Their expertise and understanding were absolutely critical in the making of this book.

Peter Martin for his friendship and wonderful photographs. He is an artist, a wizard with camera in hand. My deep thanks go out to Peter for taking this project on with me.

John Metsa and Carol Carlson, of the *Comet Theatre* in Cook, MN, for their spontaneous and warm hospitality in allowing us to use the theatre to make some photographs.

Jessica Panula for working as my typist on this book. I thank her for her excellent work, her patience with me and her upbeat spirit and warm smile.

Table of Contents

The First Snow

The first dusting of snow signals the coming of winter. The tamaracks that were bright gold just a week ago have faded to a soft brown. The light snow adorns the gray fields in a way that highlights the bare contours of the land. It is a time of the year when the ribs, clavicles, and fibulas of the terrain are exposed – no pastures of dancing green and wildflowers; not yet the peaceful blanket of winter's white. The wind comes racing down out of the empty reaches of the far north and sets the large branches of the white pines to waving a farewell to the memories of summer's brief spell.

Out in this early winter, I walk along a county road with the crazy mutt dog whose home also happens to be our home. She must somehow think it is still summer as she splashes merrily along in the dark, cold drainage ditches, oblivious to the signs of that season which has now descended upon us. For sure, there will be some milder days before land and lakes begin to freeze up, but a day like this one nevertheless reminds us that a corner has been turned, a passage has been made.

On the north side of the road, a large raven eyes us from a perch in the top of a beautiful Norway pine. The bird's feathers are ruffed up and look out of place somehow, as if this creature had been stirred too early by this blast of snow and cold. The raven is making an odd, throaty, hollow call that seems to have an internal echo all its own. As the dog and I walk, the raven flies up ahead to another perch and glances back at us earth-bound creatures as we trudge up the road toward it. I think to myself, "What on earth is that creature saying?" Though I do not speak or understand the language of ravens, I think I hear something about being still, being with others, being warmed by firewood, and being home.

Inside once more, with cup of coffee in hand, it occurs to me how we human beings get confused about happiness and contentment. The country outside today does not speak of happiness in any of the ways our culture has come to understand it, sell it and buy it. On second thought, I guess deer hunters would be happy today, because it would be good for tracking. But, by and large, happiness is commonly sold as bright blue skies and comfortable temperatures which accommodate the wearing of a new outfit, or the easy boat ride on a calm lake where the fish always bite. Much of what gets fed to us leads us to believe that happiness has everything to do with things fitting into the way we want them to be. Happiness is having it your way. Within such a blighted and unnatural perspective, contentment is down the line from happiness. Contentment has come to mean something negative – contenting yourself with less than what would make you happy. I don't think so. Contentment, rather, begins with the insight that happiness — in the sense of a wish-fulfilled personal world — is not only not realistic, but it also knocks a hole in some of those human inclinations to love others and exert care toward the world in which we live. The person who seeks happiness as his or her ultimate goal is going to be regularly slapped down by this or that disappointment or loss. A bitterness may emerge here which can color that person's life in shades of a bottomless, self-indulgent despair. Needless to say it is pretty tough to think about others, pretty tough to see the big picture from such an isolated position.

Contentment sees through happiness to a deeper place of finding oneself in the midst of a life that, thankfully, is always a mysterious dance of giving and receiving. There are so many things in our lives that we simply have no choice about at all. Some of these things are profoundly beautiful and some of them are so difficult to bear that we can hardly speak about them. And of course, much of life is lived between these extremes. When we are contented, we are able to affirm the many and varied ways that we have responded to what has

2

come to us. To be content means to be fully immersed in life and fully present to the truth that each moment is both complete unto itself and yet inevitably connected to all other moments.

Sometimes I think the birds of the sky and the creatures in the fields are better receivers of eternal truths than are we human beings, shut up behind our walls of concrete, Sheetrock and high-tech insulated windows. What was that raven saying with its persistent call and focused gaze? Was it not something about waking up to the purposefulness of all creation, and finding one's place within that web of life? Was it not something about a deep, deep trust out of which emerges an equally deep sense of contentment? I think so.

Thank You, God

Toivo and Iris were sitting in their usual spot at the Four Corners Café, right where the mid-afternoon sun graced the sturdy wooden tables with an abundance of light and warmth. The black coffee tasted good, even without the sweet rolls which they had given up a couple of years back because the doctor in Virginia told them that their cholesterol levels were too high. At least once a week, Toivo would remark to Iris and anyone else within earshot, for that matter, that he was actually glad that the lady doctor had told him to lay off the sweet rolls, because now, at age 82, he could really taste the clean, sharp, alive flavor of a good cup of coffee. Toivo's declaration was almost always followed by Iris summoning Helen out from behind the counter and telling her that she made the best coffee in all of northeastern Minnesota. And then Toivo would put an exclamation point on Iris' statement, raising his right hand, extending his index finger toward Helen and declaring with the authority, warmth and love borne of hundreds of cups of coffee consumed each year, "You betcha she does." A quiet affirmative silence would fall over the tables, chairs, and counter at the Four Corners. Mid-afternoon was generally a slow time. Iris and Toivo now enjoyed this peacefulness almost as much as they had in earlier days the hub-bub of Sunday dinner at the Four Corners, when folks came in droves after church and pushed the crew to their limits in serving up great mounds of hot-steamy roast beef, mashed potatoes and gravy. In fact, about once a month, Toivo and Iris still came in to enjoy that Sabbath feast as well as the people and all the memories stirred by the talk of their friends and neighbors.

But today was Wednesday, and it was time to head back home, north up toward Tower a ways, then cut back west and a bit south to the old homestead that had been the only home Toivo had ever known. Toivo and Iris loved riding in the big red Mercury Grand Marquis, which he had bought four or five years ago. On occasion, Toivo would acknowledge that Iris was probably right that the big Merc was too much car for them; but, he would quickly follow with an expression of his heartfelt conviction that he had worked hard all those years at Reserve Mining plus having run the farm at the same time, and it was only natural to have a little "dessert" toward the sunset of one's days. They rounded the curve next to the large tamarack swamp at the base of their long narrow driveway. Son-in-law John had been around because the strand of gravel had been freshly plowed. New snow was thrown against old snow, and the banks glittered in the dying light of day. Up ahead they saw John and their daughter Laura shoveling the walks around the farm. The three grandchildren, Erin, Jane and John, Jr. were visible helping their parents a bit, but mostly playing in the dry January snow, which had fallen the night before.

Iris put something together for supper that evening and the seven of them joined hands around the large kitchen table. By

7:30 John, Jr. had crawled into his mother's lap and fallen asleep. It was time for them to go home. Toivo walked them out to their car and said goodnight. Iris waved from behind the kitchen door. Then Toivo sauntered down the driveway as far as the creek to work off a little of mother's cooking, as he put it. The night was ever so still and deep. The constellations wheeled overhead.

Toivo headed back up the drive to the house. He glanced up at a bedroom window on the second floor and through the frosted glass he could see Iris standing in front of the mirror, combing out her long beautiful, silver-gray hair. To him she was every bit as lovely as she was some 60 years ago. Into the house and down into the basement, Toivo loaded up the woodstove with an armful of well-cured maple. He paused, feeling the warmth and whispered under his breath, "Thank you, God."

Joy in the Barking

The days are getting longer now. Last Friday evening it was 6:00 p.m., I was out tramping along a country road, and it was still light. The sun was just slipping over the horizon. The sky was a pretty, almost royal blue, and in the east a big, round, orange moon was peeking out around a stand of jack pines. My crazy dog, Hudeatch, ran ahead of me – leaping here and there, scooting under fences, and burying her head in the snow – undoubtedly in search of some tasty field mice as appetizers prior to a full bowl of Purina.

When I was a dog, I mean child, we always had dogs. There was Fritzi, the Spitz mix, who followed my brother home from kindergarten. There was Betsy, the Basset/Beagle mix, from up in the north Georgia mountains. There was Ranger, whose ability to launch herself vertically was so impressive that kids came from all over the neighborhood to watch the show. There was Prince, the regal but stupid Collie/Shepherd mix. There was the dog saint of my childhood, the magnificent Bismarck, who was also a Collie/Shepherd mix. Bismarck and I played many a tackle football game under the stars on soft fall nights. And then there was our first "child", a New Hampshire bred canine of Lab, Belgian Shepherd and Border Collie heritage. This was Marpa, named for a Tibetan sage. She spent her early years on the campus of a boarding school where she was adored, not only by her "parents" but by many students as well.

And now for almost the last eight years, there has been Hudeatch – that's Slovenian for Little Devil. What a name for a dog that belongs to a couple of ministers. Hudeatch came into our family clearly as the result of unresolved grief on my part. Within a week after Marpa died, I had to have another dog. So the little notice in the paper said "sheepdog/lab mix." Well, Marpa was part Lab. That sounded good. When I went out to Ely Lake and saw these puppies, there were several black and white ones, just like Marpa. There was no stopping me now. When the rest of the family came out to inspect the litter, they generally preferred a couple of the more sedate black and tan puppies. Oh no, to my mind, it had to be that exuberant, shall I say, wildly exuberant black and white one. And so it was that the most grief-stricken family member was allowed to choose the hyper-kinetic black and white puppy to whom we gave a name that would be prophetic: Hudeatch. This dog turned out to be truly everything that Marpa was not. Hudeatch was clumsy right from the start and has stayed that way. Hudeatch almost never settles down. She will stand and pant for an hour straight before she finally lies down. And then she continues to pant lying down. The vet says no problem with the panting. It's just Hudeatch. It's annoying to be reading, eating, watching television and have this dog close by panting heavily. In the old days, perfect strangers would come up to us and look at Marpa and say things like, "Oh my that's the prettiest dog." It is

inconceivable that this could ever happen with Hudeatch. Hudeatch has a sheepdog muzzle with the fuzz hanging down from her lower jaw. It's always dirty from who knows what, and she pretty much looks like she's got a permanent chewing tobacco stain on her chin. We used to say she'd be a pretty nice-looking dog with a head transplant.

And then there's her behavior. We soon found out that any food left out on the table counter — even the garbage — Hudeatch considered fair game. Many the times there have been, when we arrived home to find garbage strewn about the kitchen and a sheepish Hudeatch with coffee grounds stuck to her muzzle. I could go on and on, but let me move now to some of the lessons that we have learned these last eight years with Hudeatch.

It was my wife who first pointed out that the Creator had sent Hudeatch to us to make us more humble. To which I replied, "Yeah, right!" But over the years I have come to get the mes-

sage. Hudeatch, despite some of her obviously less than desirable characteristics, is a creature of God's own making. We chose her, well I chose her, and in doing so, assumed responsibility for taking care of one of God's critters. She's unruly and not very attractive. She's got bad breath, and she'll drool on you in an instant. She's an "in your face" kind of beast who rests only when she's actually fallen asleep. But she is ours. In her own strange kind of way, she's bonded with us. She thinks of us as her family, which in and of itself raises the issue of us being humbled. And equally strangely, out of this humility there has grown a begrudging sense of affection for this ratty, bedraggled-looking dog who never knew that she would be asked to fill the paws of a family canine legend, Marpa.

Sometimes these days, when I go out walking with Hudeatch, I take a lot of joy watching her race wildly through the snow, the brush and drainage ditches. She's in her glory. She's a happy dog! That's some kind of lesson there: that there is joy to be found in another's joy – that joy is not always about having the world give to you in the ways that you wish for. Sometimes joy is something you have to work at finding. And from time to time life throws a Hudeatch at us to challenge us to grow – to deepen and broaden our appreciation for the earth and all the creatures therein. Sometimes it seems we're given what we don't ask for and asked to grow from that.

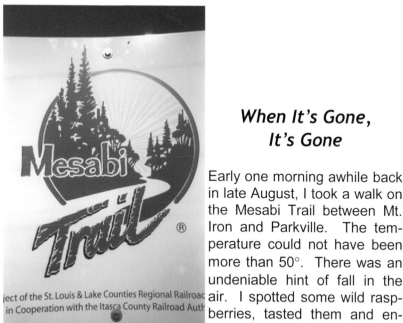

ject of the St. Louis & Lake Counties Regional Railroad
in Cooperation with the Itasca County Railroad Auth

When It's Gone, It's Gone

Early one morning awhile back in late August, I took a walk on the Mesabi Trail between Mt. Iron and Parkville. The temperature could not have been more than 50°. There was an undeniable hint of fall in the air. I spotted some wild raspberries, tasted them and enjoyed the tart-sweet flavor. Chokecherries were starting to ripen into a full rich burgundy color. Big, bold splashes of goldenrod painted the woods with the promise of the still brighter scarlet of maples in the full splendor of late September. In the western sky an almost full moon hung suspended like a pale, slightly smudged silver dollar. In the low places, the wild smell of balsam and popple rose up sharply into my nostrils and filled me with an edgy, heady excitement that is both familiar and mysterious to me.

Awhile later, I found myself alternately sipping a cup of green tea and chewing on a piece of rye toast. On the television was The Weather Channel. On the screen there was revealed a stretch of interstate highway that runs right through downtown Atlanta. Not so very long ago (thirty years or so) that road had but two lanes in each direction. Now that same piece of highway has five lanes in each direction. Some, probably most, call it progress. The weather people were busily babbling, alerting us to the fact that Atlanta is under a Code Red smog

alert today. People with heart problems, asthma and other up-
per respiratory difficulties are urged to stay indoors in air-
conditioned environments. The expected high in "Hotlanta" on
this day in late summer is 98°.

And I almost forgot to mention that Atlanta is in the midst of a
major drought. Outdoor watering has been dramatically cur-
tailed and, in some areas, banned altogether. The city's main
supply of water is the Chattahoochee River, a beautiful stream
that comes rollicking out of the Blue Ridge Mountains to the
north and rolls all the way to the Gulf of Mexico (though it takes
a different name once it crosses the Florida line). It's been
said that Coca Cola bottled in Atlanta tastes better than anywhere else because the water comes out of the Chattahoochee. Well the Chattahoochee is singing a pretty dry,
wispy tune these days as the effects of the drought take their
toll. There are no aquifers – vast underground reservoirs of
water – to bail out the city that is rapidly earning the reputation
as the southeastern version of Los Angeles. I suppose this
kind of doom-saying might be taken as a skewed form of nos-
talgia – a native son remembering his hometown as the sim-
pler, more livable place than it had been in the not so distant
past. But let me go just a bit further.

A couple of weeks ago, I
read a local newspaper
article about a proposed
development of a remote
lake northwest of Elbow
Lake, which is of course
hard by the western end of
Vermilion. Yes, we're
back in northeastern Min-
nesota now. The article
explained that there are a
few cabins on this lake on
leased land. Apparently a
developer from outside the
area wants to purchase

these spots, and develop them into full-blown home sites. According to the article I read, access to this lake is difficult, which has allowed the area to retain its rustic, relatively pristine character. If this developer has his way, the future of this little piece of northern Minnesota will change dramatically and some will call it progress.

Now I am very clear that my roots are grafted into the rock and duff and clay of northern Minnesota. This is my adopted home, and I am an adopted son to this majestic land. In the local vernacular, I am a "packsacker", an outsider, and I always will be. But I have lived here long enough to know that northeastern Minnesota is a gem – its land and its people. I believe we who live here have a connection to our place, that is absolutely priceless. We are connected to our jobs, our land and each other in ways that are a distant memory for many parts of the country. We pick wild berries in the woods. Many cut their own firewood to keep warm in the winter months. Lots of folks are employed in jobs that link them to the resources of the land, and there is an honesty and straightforwardness that comes from hard outdoor work. In town and out in the country, we have gardens that nourish us with fresh produce and delight us with beautiful flowers. We know our neighbors and, when adversity rears its head, people know how to pitch in and take care of each other. Our region is one in which people are in touch with family and cultural traditions in ways that link them to their past and provide continuity with the future. It is true that many young people leave to find work. It is also true that many return as soon as work opens up here.

I could go on, but my point is that, somehow in our area, there yet exists a kind of scale – a balance of forces that overall makes for a good way of life for the majority of people. At the risk of sounding like a voice crying in the wilderness, I believe that we are coming into a time that will test this balanced scale of life which probably most of us have come to take for granted. The same forces that have transformed my hometown Atlanta from a comfortable mid-sized city into a sprawling (for many unworkable) megalopolis are at work everywhere.

Change is inevitable. Change can be very good, or change can be devastating. What is unfolding regarding development on that lake west of Elbow Lake is symbolic of what we are likely to be facing in many places around our area in the near future. We are going to be called upon to make decisions about what kind of development we want in northeastern Minnesota. In thinking about these issues, we need to reflect ever so seriously on what we already have been given – this almost uncanny balance between human beings and their environment on this northern frontier. We are going to make decisions that will either serve to keep this precious balance intact for those who follow us or, instead, lead us down the path to becoming like those other places with such visible signs of "success" as more traffic, more fast food restaurants, outlet malls, and less open space for everyone.

Is growth bad? Of course not. Is development bad? Of course not. It all depends on how these issues are managed so as to maintain a balance in which human community can be nourished in body, mind and spirit. In the book of Genesis, we are told that God placed human beings in the critical role of being stewards over all that the Creator made. Over the centuries, there have been times and places where humans have done better and worse jobs on this. For this particular pilgrim out on a late summer stroll through the forest, it is not difficult to see the preciousness of what we have here in northern Minnesota. We find this preciousness in our personal dealings with the people who make their livelihoods selling us the things we need for our lives. We find this preciousness in a way of living that is focused on the outdoors – of knowing the peace of living on a lake or regularly spending time on one. We find this preciousness in sensing that we are part of our environment, not separate from it.

We have so much to be thankful for, but stewardship requires vigilance, action and serious reflection on the responsibilities which God has given us in our particular place and for our particular time. We can be sure that in the years ahead there will be lots of pressure on our area to get in lock step and become like those other "successful" places. We need to remember the birthright that we have been given and define success on our own terms in a way that maintains that balance – that harmony . . . that peace . . . that integrity that we all recognize and love in our part of the world.

Growing up, my father used to take my brother and me on fishing trips. In the morning, we would load the cooler up with Cokes, sandwiches and other goodies. Well, ten o'clock would often find me rummaging around with the cooler, getting started on the food and drink. Usually we fished all day, not going in at lunch, and so when my old Pa would see me working my way through the Cokes, sandwiches, chips and cookies he would say "Son, easy does it. When it's gone, it's gone." When I think about the life we have here and some of the challenges we are and will be facing, those same words come to mind in a much more heightened way than whether or not the last sandwich has been eaten and it's only 11:00 a.m. When you want to get your lawn mower fixed, but there's no small engine repair shop in town, but only a mall where you can buy a

new one, it'll be too late then. When the last locally owned café has closed its doors and the only place you can get a stack of pancakes is some chain restaurant out of Kansas City, it'll be too late then. When the peace of your spot on the lake has been drowned out by activities at some newly opened Wisconsin Dells style theme park and beach resort, it will be too late then. Because when it's gone, it's gone.

Up here under the northern sky, history, diverse cultures and the earth itself have created a people of strength and integrity. The bonds that connect us with each other, with the land, and with history are ultimately spiritual ones. They are from God, and they make us who we are and who we may yet become. If we forget the sacred character of these ties that bind and treat them instead as commodities to be bought and sold at the marketplace, then we do so at our own peril and that of our children and grandchildren.

Surprise!

In the far northwestern corner of St. Louis County, there lies an expanse of wide open country that is well described as being the back of beyond. This piece of country is way off the Highway 53 corridor with its relentless flow of summer traffic. St. Louis, Koochiching and Itasca Counties all converge in a dramatically quiet way with old barns scattered about the popple-clad hills overlooking the valley of the Littlefork River.

Yevgeny was a Russian exchange student, who had come to northern Minnesota to meet his girlfriend's family in Orr. They had met at the University of Minnesota, where Yevgeny was pursuing a degree in Political Science and Anna was enrolled in the pre-med course of study. Now, as the two of them drove west out of Greaney, Yevgeny remarked on how beautiful the countryside was. He told Anna that the landscape was similar to that around his home village in the northwest part of Russia. Yevgeny acknowledged that it actually made him a little homesick to see the spruce spires standing up tall and straight into the bright blue northern sky. Anna said that she didn't want Yevgeny to be sad. She wanted to show him some beautiful country that she had hoped would be a comfort to him, and give him a sense of familiarity in a place very far from his own home. Anna further explained, in a very dear and philosophical way, that it had often seemed to her that a person does not truly understand the depth and power of the familiar until it is experienced within the context of that which is unfamiliar. Anna's beginning level of Russian was good enough that she made Yevgeny understand the subtlety of her point. He smiled brightly at her as they descended to the crossing of the Littlefork at a place called Samuelson Park.

Anna was talkative as the car sped across the bridge. She told Yevgeny about floating down the Littlefork as a child with her parents and her two brothers, and how they frequently stopped right at Samuelson Park to fry up their catch of fish. She waxed poetically about the beauty of the river with its thick stands of cedar and abundant wildlife. She talked at length about the people who had started the sheep farm just up river and how they kept losing their animals to wolves – until they invested in some fearsome Hungarian sheepdogs that put the wolves in their place. Yevgeny heard Anna talking, but he had to a great extent become lost in his own thoughts.

Yevgeny found himself musing about why he had come to Minnesota in the first place. This line of thought led him to images from his youth, which now floated quite clearly before his mind's eye. Life had been somewhat gray in an overall sort of way in his home village deep in the Russian taiga. Yevgeny was not a child of the Gorbachev "revolution". He had grown up during the times when the state's influence was everywhere. But despite the gray on the surface of things, the fires of home and family in his northern village continued to sustain and inspire its residents. Yevgeny remembered the depth of his parents' faith and the occasional secret religious services that the family was able to attend. He remembered seeing the tears roll down his mother's cheeks as the Orthodox priest distributed the Communion meal to those gathered behind tightly shuttered windows or in a candlelit cellar.

Anna continued to share her own memories as the two of them swept along out of the valley and up on to some higher ground. There on the left side of the road in a place called Bramble, there rose up a sight that shocked Yevgeny out of his reverie. He was so surprised by what he saw that he could barely get the words out to tell Anna to pull over to the side of the road and stop the car. Set just back off the road – and framed by a field stretching toward the west – was a small Russian Orthodox church with it's characteristic onion dome steeple pressing toward the heavens out of the green north country earth.

Transfixed, Yevgeny got out of Anna's well-worn VW Rabbit and walked across the road toward the church. In front of the church was a high archway. In the beam across the top of the arch the word **Joy** was engraved with great simplicity and purposefulness. A light breeze ruffled the leaves and blew them across the little churchyard. Yevgeny stepped under the arch into a sacred space and time. He moved slowly toward the entrance to the church and then stopped. Yevgeny knelt down and allowed his forehead to rest on the cool dark soil. The images, which only moments before had been so vivid on the screen of his consciousness, were suddenly gone.

Instead, Yevgeny was very much aware of the here and the now, in an overpowering sort of way that was nevertheless completely unthreatening. The dirt and the grass smelled good. The sun on his neck was marvelously warm and comforting. The birds sang their delicate anthems in the nearby trees. Yevgeny could not believe that here, thousands of miles from the village where he grew up, he could understand so clearly what it meant to come home.

The sun was beginning to set by the time Yevgeny got up, dusted himself off, and stood in the middle of that little Russian Orthodox churchyard, once again staring at the incongruity of the onion dome amid the popples, jack pines and hayfields of Bramble, Minnesota. Anna was still sitting in the driver's seat when Yevgeny made his way back to the car. He sat down

and blurted out in Russian, a few words of amazement about what had just happened to him. Anna put her index finger to her lips and shook her head. Yevgeny understood there was no need to try and explain. Anna cranked up the reliable little VW and pointed it toward home. Yevgeny rested peacefully, even blissfully, in the passenger seat.

When they pulled into the driveway at Anna's home, Yevgeny didn't stir and Anna didn't wake him. He slept all night in the Rabbit. He woke up only once and found the Big Dipper and then the North Star. As he drifted off to sleep once more, Yevgeny saw the church in Bramble very clearly and the feelings of peace he had known in the afternoon came over him again. And then he slept. Yevgeny was home.

Up North at Easter

It was late February, for the last couple of days a warm wind out of the southwest had blown steadily. It was as if a little bit of Texas or Arizona had come to northern Minnesota for a brief visit. There was mighty melting everywhere. Jack sat in the kitchen of the sturdy little cabin, drinking lots of coffee and watching the drip turn to drip, drip to drip, drip, drip to almost a stream of water rolling down the steep-pitched roof. He knew that weather like this made many people in the area quite happy. They would start talking about spring, and baseball and opening their lake cabins. It never ceased to amaze Jack that people could talk such foolishness when the fierce storms of March had not even yet begun to sweep over the lakes and forests. "People can be pretty stupid," Jack thought to himself.

It had been a long winter for Jack. Come the middle of March, it would be one year that Jack had been a widower. Summer had not been too bad. There was so much to do around the place in the warm weather. He had patched the roof and repaired the little deck on the backside of the cabin. Martha had been after him for two years to put some new boards in that deck and reinforce the railing. Well, he finally got around to it, and she wasn't there to see the results of his efforts. His son and daughter had come up from the Cities in July with their families. For almost two weeks there was energy and joy and hope dashing around Jack's world in the flying feet and smiling faces of his six grandchildren. Jack got up early every morning while they were there and prepared huge breakfasts – his secret recipe buttermilk pancakes, big meaty slabs of bacon, maple syrup from the trees on his 80 acres, and fresh-squeezed orange juice. His children and his son-in-law and daughter-in-law were good to him with a deep gentle kindness, even if they never could find quite the right words when Martha's name came up.

In the fall, Jack spent as much time as he could partridge hunting. Honey, the golden Lab, was as sweet a dog as God ever made. There were days in October and early November when Jack and Honey would leave the cabin before the sun came up and not return until after sundown. The bright blue October light, blending with the golden hillsides of popple, was soothing to Jack's broken heart. Sometimes, when he would stop for lunch, the tears would begin to flow. Honey always noticed this and would sidle up next to Jack and make every effort to lick the tears off his cheeks.

A big Thanksgiving blizzard roared in and prevented the planned family gathering. Jack was alone that day. As the winter set in with some seriousness, Jack's solitude deepened. He fed the birds; and their fearless persistence impressed and amused him. Honey spent a lot of the time a few feet back from the woodstove, grunting contentedly and enjoying the quiet companionship of a good master. Jack's place was quite a ways off the beaten path on a county road, and then another quarter mile in on a driveway that he and Martha had done most of the work on themselves. A neighbor down the way kept Jack plowed out and would occasionally stop in to see how he was doing. But basically Jack spent the winter pretty much by himself with Honey, the birds and a lifetime of memories.

Even after Jack had seen some videos of recent family gatherings made by his daughter Jane, he wasn't all that impressed. He preferred the photographs that Martha had lovingly and laboriously enshrined in some 15 albums that were neatly arranged in the bookshelf that Jack himself had made. As the winter dragged on, Jack would find himself beginning to look through those photograph albums. It might be well after midnight and there Jack would sit – staring into the well of his own history: the faces, the gatherings, the places, the people. Gradually, he let all of it begin to sink in; and as he did, there surfaced in his heart – in the silence of those winter nights – the most tender feelings of acceptance: an affirmation of the light – a love for all that had unfolded in their journey together. There was a photograph of him and Martha and Jane and Bill when they were all very young. The kids, Jack figured, must have been about five and eight when the picture was taken. Jack remembered the trip – a canoeing adventure in the country off to the north of Grand Marais. On the way home they stopped in Grand Marais, and walked out on the point there that juts into Lake Superior. Jack asked a passerby to snap off a shot of them standing next to the big lake. The person was cooperative and the old Kodak box camera did the rest. And there they were, faces bright and glowing, shining life right through that black and white medium. The big inland sea sprawled out to eternity in the background. Jack took this picture out of the album, and he taped it right in the kitchen window so he could see it when he washed dishes. He liked looking at the picture. It made him feel good and hopeful.

Well, the storms of March did come, and one blustery afternoon a letter arrived from Jane. She had been talking with Bill and they had decided they wanted to come north for Easter.

That would be different. In earlier years, when Martha was still living, she and Jack were often in Arizona or New Mexico at Easter time. There would be some nice phone calls with the family, and some laughter about snow still being on the ground in Minnesota while they dined outdoors with the smell of flowers blooming. Jack eyed the letter from Jane – coming north for Easter. "That certainly would be different," he said out loud.

Jack looked at the black and white photograph on the kitchen window, then glanced back at the letter from Jane, and then toward the row of white pines straining under the weight of the March wind. The snow had stopped falling, and the sun was actually starting to come out. Jack mused, "What a great idea. Everybody up north at Easter." And then it was as if Jack had stepped through a window in time. For the first time all winter Jack began to think about spring.

As he lay down to sleep that evening, Jack was filled with the most positive anticipation about everyone being up north at Easter. He still felt the pain of his loss, but for the first time since Martha's death, the pain was truly also intermingled with all the goodness of their life together. In that intermingling, Jack sensed that something good was happening. In that intermingling Jack felt new life. And in the quiet of the night before sleep descended, Jack experienced a spirit of gratitude that was new to him, unlike anything he had ever known before.

Now is the Time

Most all the leaves have fallen and the hillsides are gray and bare. A few tamaracks deep in the swamp hold on stubbornly to their golden needles. But with the high wind we had over-night, I suspect their branches have mostly been swept clean by now. The waters of the Rice River looked dark and cold the other day, warm blue summer days just a memory now. And it's cold. The forecast calls for 18° on Saturday night. Winter cannot be too far away now. It is a time of quiet waiting – the earth still and peaceful with a blanket of leaves and needles pulled up over its bare shoulders. I picture a big furry black bear rolled into a ball, dug in under the soft soil of an uprooted tree, snoring and snuffling, and resting up for another year of life.

This is a season of muted tones, of browns and grays in many different shades. It is a subtle season of moods that heave and shift: making us one day pensive, feeling acutely the loss of summer's warm days and autumn's bright colors, while find-ing us the next day quietly but eagerly anticipating the beauty of winter's first snowfall. Something is happening to us amidst the darkening gloom of November. There is a magical shud-dering in our bones that takes us back to ancestral campfires from eons ago. We know in the core of our flesh and spirit that it is a time to let the season take us to a deeper, more abiding place.

Outside my window the sky spits some tiny blips of snow. It won't amount to anything, just a reminder that there is no turn-ing back now. And this is good. It is comforting to know that winter would come whether I wanted it to or not. That's part of the meaning of the season. It reminds us that the obvious beauty of summer withers and fades into the damp, cold molding mustiness of November. It's okay. It's good. It means that life is given. It means that our lives are gifts. Next time the cold wind blows you down the street give thanks to God. Think of that wind as the Creator's breath that energizes you and all other living things.

God created the natural world as a great fullness of good and order and purpose. God gave us the capacity to feel this living power in creation. But all too often we cut ourselves off from these vibrant forces. We neglect the opportunity to walk with the Creator in the slanting rays of an early winter sunset. We fail to acknowledge the "wake up to life" call of a cold rain that stings our faces. We fear the closing of highways in a winter blizzard, when we could instead rejoice in the opportunity to spend a restful day at home. There is a goodness in all of nature that God has placed there for our enjoyment and for the deepening of our spirits if we would but take the time to see these truths.

Now is the time. Now is the time to rejoice in the gray of November. Now is the time to see the Creator's breath blowing the leaves wildly down the street and across the yards and way off into the fields and forests. Now is the time to be still. Now is the time.

Sweet Old Boots

It hit me like a dreamy ton of bricks made out of polar fleece. It was like the muffled downy sound of a Canadian Jay floating out of a white pine to attend to business at the bird feeder. It was a kind of revelation in the familiar as I put on my Sorel boots for the first time this winter.

It happened a couple of weeks ago. A great big snowstorm had been predicted, and I was feeling as frisky as a bird dog on opening day. But instead of a winter wonderland, we got several inches of wet gloppy snow, much of which melted right on down into the dark, sleepy November earth. Well, despite being disappointed by this pathetic attempt at a storm, I decided I would go out into the night anyway and take enjoyment in the dark and the quiet.

So, I dug out my Sorels, sat on the couch and proceeded to put them on. And as I said before, when I slipped my size thirteen flippers into those cozy felt liners, it was like I was suddenly enveloped by a cloud of déjà vu that collapsed the memories of winters gone by into a single, exquisite moment of appreciation for the past, anticipation of the future, and wonder in the brightly shining present. But actually, it was quite a bit more straightforward than all that. It just felt good to have those big funny looking boots on again. It never ceases to amaze me how Sorels will keep your feet warm even in the most bitter cold. Your face may be freezing, but if you've got your Sorels on, your feet will be toasty warm.

The first time I ever saw Sorel boots was when we were living in northern New Hampshire where it can get pretty cold, too. I thought to myself "Man, those are some seriously ugly boots." I didn't know then how unbelievably warm those boots could keep your feet, even with temperatures well below zero. Some years back, when I worked at a mental health center in Wisconsin, the clinical director there, a very fine psychiatrist, used to wear his Sorel boots all winter. He would wear them right through the workday, sitting there with those ugly boots and bright yellow laces. It certainly did not have a negative impact on his practice, because there was a steady stream of clients that came to see him all week.

My wife has, for most of our marriage, complained about cold hands and feet. Several years into our marriage, I convinced her that during the winter months she ought to wear socks to bed at night. Before she adopted the habit, many were the nights when her cold feet on my warm feet woke me out of a nice, sound, wintry sleep. A pair of socks solved the nighttime problem. For the daytime concerns, I gave her for Christmas an enormous calf length pair of Sorel boots. They were lavender with a design of a polar bear on the back part of the heel. I loved them! Kristin gulped a bit when she opened the package, but she wore them faithfully for many winters until just a couple of years ago when I got her an even more imposing pair of Sorels – heavier soles, all black with the look of polar expedition gear. If the Oakland Raiders played football in Alaska this would be their footwear. This time she laughed with great enthusiasm, and she has worn them regularly when the weather called for serious foot warmth which, for her, is all winter.

So, it is amazing what can come from just one little moment of slipping on a pair of boots for the first time of the winter. A moment like that is pregnant with memories and people and hopes and dreams. It is easy to lose touch with the preciousness of each moment. For much of our life, we may look at time as an enemy that keeps getting in the way of our ability to do all the things we feel we have to do. An excitable and quite verbose college professor of mine used to describe this predicament as the "economics of the scarcity of temporality." We just shook our heads.

Every moment in life is connected to all others. When we are open to this truth, our lives are enriched. There is a bright light that surrounds this awareness. The Creator calls us to wake from the dullness of self-absorption. The extraordinary is always there pulsing through the rhythms of what our haste leads us to deem as ordinary.

New Life

Almost three years ago, we went to visit my family at Easter. On Saturday night, before we left for Atlanta on Easter evening, my mother called and said that my father was in the hospital and would probably have to have angioplasty. It would not be a big deal, and we would probably all still get to spend some time in the mountains toward the end of the week. Once we got to Atlanta, more data had been collected and it turned out my father's condition was quite a bit more serious than first thought. He was going to have to go through major heart surgery to have any chance of returning to a robust quality of life. If he did not have surgery he would end up in a nursing home, on oxygen, and likely waste away in a year or so. The non-surgical option was never anything he considered. He wanted to take the shot at having some good years, even though he was well aware that the odds were stacked pretty high against him.

On the day surgery was scheduled, it was later in the morning when the nurses came and took my father to the operating room. It was the last time I saw him alive. As always, he was laughing and teasing with people. I know he was scared, but somehow he was always able to change fear into energy and motivation to meet the challenge before him. He didn't, even at the gravest of moments, let fear stand in his way. As he waved goodbye with a big, confident smile, we all felt somehow that this would be another battle that he would find a way to win. Well, it didn't go that way. His heart was too badly damaged; and when the repairs were completed, there just wasn't enough juice left in the battery to crank the engine. He was on life support for a couple of days; which I think was a couple of days too long, because it was clear that, following surgery and despite the best efforts of a fine team of doctors and nurses, my father wasn't going to make it.

The days after his death were blue and none of what had happened seemed very real. However, it was all very real. In the months that followed, I caught myself many times thinking of something I wanted to talk to my father about, and then realizing that he wasn't there. The following fall the University of Georgia football team went 10 and 2, and there was a palpable ache in my heart in not being able to re-hash the games by telephone with my father on Saturday nights. That's something we had done every year since I went off to college at age 19. Now my brother and I do the post-game discussion, and that's good too. My grief has not been a soul-shaking one that has led me into teary swamps of sadness. But there have been many times in the last three years, when I have missed my father a great deal. He was honest, smart, perceptive, and he had a will so strong that it always made us feel he could accomplish anything he really set his mind to. And he pretty much did. He faced death with a lot of courage and with the same buoyancy with which he lived his whole life.

I know grieving is different for each one of us for a variety of reasons. We're all different people and our relationships with our loved ones have their own unique characteristics. None of our loved ones is perfect, and death doesn't change that. But in the grieving, I think we are able, through the power of absence, to extract that person's presence in a new, powerful and ultimately healing way.

Grieving helps us to recollect all the ways that our loved one had an impact on us. Our grief points out to us the manner in which that person has shaped who we are and who we will become. The person who has died lives on in us through our values, the choices we make, the hopes and dreams which light our way, and in the very substance of our flesh and blood. The continuity of life and the meaningfulness of this continuity become paramount during a time of grieving.

What does this mean? Well, it means a lot of things. It means that your grief is healing – that if you let yourself go through it fully, you will be joined forever to your loved one at levels so rich and deep, that you could not have imagined them being possible during your worst days of grief. Going through grief will wind up renewing your life, waking you up to some of the adventure of life, which had perhaps been worn away by your routines. Finally, it is through walking the lonesome valley that we have the opportunity to discover firsthand that love really is stronger than death. Without loss, without grieving then this truth would remain an intellectual construct that makes for good discussion, but lacks the power to transform lives. My father's been gone almost three years now, but I truly have never been more aware of how much he is and will remain a part of my life.

Fred and Lola

I look at them as carefully as I am able to out of the corner of my right eye. I certainly do not want to be staring at them. Well, at least I do not want them to notice that I am trying to get a good close look at them. They appear to be in their seventies, both carrying a few extra pounds. She must dye her hair because it is absolutely jet black in color. He does not have much of anything on his head but sunburned skin. I decide to think of them as Lola and Fred. They are there leaning against each other in the clinic waiting room. There is a sweetness and coziness about Fred and Lola that is quite visible, even with just the pinched gaze that I am able to direct toward them. His head is thrown back slightly, as he snores in the gentle purring fashion of a peaceful pussycat sunning himself next to a window with the curtains drawn back. Lola's head is cocked forward as it rests gently on Fred's shoulder. Her eyes are closed. There is a tautness in her neck and arms that indicates she is probably more just resting her eyes than actually sleeping.

All of a sudden it jumps out at me like a child knocking over a glass of milk on the dining room table – their hands. Her tiny little left hand, which is weighed down with a couple of blocky silver rings and a turquoise bracelet (looks like she's been to Santa Fe, I muse) rests on his gray trousered knee. On top of and actually swallowing up her hand is his somewhat corpulent bear paw of a hand. It is big and red, the backside covered with sun bleached blond hair. His hand and hers are locked in a tight embrace even as he snores the minutes away, waiting for the nurse to call out the name that will re-focus their attention on why they are sitting there in the clinic waiting room.

I begin to wonder which one of them is sick. Actually neither of them looks sick, though Fred would probably look a little better if his mouth were closed. I turn my head and look at them more directly. I stare momentarily, and quickly conclude that they are from Minnesota, but that they spend their winters in the southwest somewhere. Perhaps Lola senses my gaze because she lifts her head from Fred's shoulder, turns my way and smiles. It is a sweet, warm smile and our eyes connect. I also smile and turn away feeling mildly embarrassed, sensing that perhaps she knew I was staring at them.

I hear Fred stirring, rustling a newspaper in his lap. I want to turn and look, but I don't. I hear them talking now. The appointment is still an hour and a half away. He wants to go get something to eat. She wants to stay put in case they get called earlier. There is no real disagreement in their voices, just the stating of preferences. I clear my throat and turn their way as if I were just re-adjusting my seated position. Amazingly their hands are still clasped together – his big ham hock around her small silver and turquoise encrusted hand. I begin to have this odd sense of being touched by this couple. They don't look nervous or afraid. Their hands look like they've actually melded together and become a shared anatomical part. My mind runs on – hoping that neither one of them is terribly ill. They seem so happy. They seem so at ease and comfortable with each other. And their hands – I can't get over their hands. Some renaissance master painter should walk out of the mists and paint Fred and Lola's hands clasped together.

The reverie is broken when a particular name is called. Fred and Lola get up as one. A nurse enters the waiting room pushing a rather fancy wheelchair in which a man in his thirties, perhaps early forties is seated. The man obviously has some sort of motor problem and probably a whole lot more. His head bobs arhythmically and his tongue hangs limply from the corner of this mouth. The man's arms move up and down in a definite twitchy fashion. He attempts to form words when he sees Fred and Lola coming toward him and his lips curl up into a smile.

44

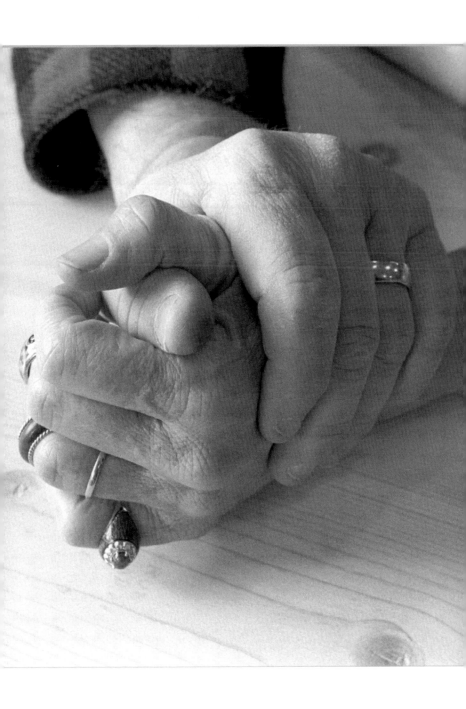

Like a bolt of lightning at dawn it hits me. Fred and Lola aren't sick at all. The man in the wheelchair must be their son. Fred and Lola are still holding hands as they kneel in front of the man in the wheelchair. They speak softly to him with great tenderness. The man breaks into a huge smile and swings his head around in a way that can only mean joy. I see that Fred and Lola are smiling too. I marvel at the fact that his left hand and her right are still together even as they balance squatting down next to their son.

Fred and Lola stand up and talk briefly with the nurse. The nurse leaves and the three of them remain. Fred and Lola are holding hands, talking softly to their son.

Life as It Is

The day after Christmas, I went for a walk on a county road about 30 miles north of Virginia. I was wearing jeans, a wool shirt, a windbreaker, and tennis shoes, and I was toasty warm. The sky that afternoon was a gently warm Carolina Blue, not at all the sharp, steely cold blue of late December in northern Minnesota. The shoulder of the road was soft from the warm sun that had been shining on it. In the shade of the spruce and popple, there was some crusty snow, but in the fields and in the yards around farmhouses there were huge bare patches of ground, giant tears in the fabric of what winter is supposed to be like here in our part of the world. The late afternoon sun angled in from the west, casting a sleepy, summer-like, golden glow over the brown, sleeping fields and marshes.

As I walked toward the setting sun, a light southern breeze caressed my face and there was, for just a moment, a quiver in my being accepting this anomalous spell of warm weather at a time when we ought to be gripped in the midst of winter's snowy bright beauty. I love the cold of winter. I love the fury of its icy blast. Bring it on, north wind, fill my beard with snow, and try to blow the woolen cap from my head. Let it snow until we think it cannot snow ever again, and then let it snow more until all is hushed with the deep silence of the northern winter.

But the moment of giving way to what is had already occurred. My sneaker-clad feet squished through moist gray glop and my thoughts drifted to a couple of summers ago. Actually, I think we had two years in a row when fall came to spend the summer in northern Minnesota. There are certainly discernible patterns in the nature of the world and of life itself. Regularity seems at times to rule. But that regularity does give way at times to events and patterns that do not fit the mold, that do not meet our expectations. Or, maybe, it is that there are longer term rhythms that we do not see because of the shortsightedness of our vision. Or, yet again, perhaps our vulnerability as human beings creates in us a craving for order and control in the midst of the vastness of time and space.

Lots of thoughts I thought. Maybe some years God just does something different. If God wants it to be like April in northern Minnesota instead of December, which our calendar says it is, then maybe that's just the way it is. If that's the way God wants it this year, far be it from me to argue about it. I mean after all, just because there's not much snow on the ground, that doesn't mean there's not lots of things to do, projects to complete, interests to be pursued, dreams to dream, people to love and care about.

Actually, now that I think about it, this whole business about the current warm spell is kind of reassuring. We spend a lot of times in our lives wishing for things to be a certain way for us and feeling hurt and downhearted when things don't work out the way we want them to. **God's call to us is an invitation into life as it is!** God never tells us that life is always going to be just like we want it to be. God just reminds us that as we follow the light, we will never be alone. So when things don't work out like we expect them to, we actually stand on the edge of an opportunity to embrace more of the life which God has given to us. I haven't yet started to look around the house for last summer's suntan lotion, but if it hits 50 degrees in the next day or so, I am thinking about digging out some hiking shorts and t-shirts.

Autumn: Reflection and Action

It is still August, but not for much longer. The nights are getting noticeably cooler, and the days are beginning to take on that look of crystalline blue in the bright sunshine of late summer. As you drive along in the countryside, look out your car window into the low boggy areas. It is hard to believe that only a few months ago, the floor of the forest in those places was covered with marsh marigolds. Now, as August slides gracefully toward September, one's vision is drawn upward into the leafy branches of the black ash that grow well in those damp forest places. Already, the gold fire of autumn has begun to burn its brilliant way through the lush green of summer. Black ash are the last trees to put on their leaves in the spring and the first ones to drop them in the fall. What a mystery that so much life could be compressed into a few short months.

Fall is a wondrous mix of glorious sun-filled afternoons that almost give the false message that this golden season will never come to an end, combined with brisk, chilly mornings scented with wood smoke from the home down the road whose owner heats with birch, oak and maple. One day fall tells us to stay by the lake all day and enjoy fully the achingly beautiful sweep of water, sky, rock and forest. The next day the wind swings around from the north with a jolt of cool air that heralds what lies ahead. Part of the beauty of the fall is just this pendulum swinging from quiet late summer stillness to the early turbulence of the season of cold which is yet to be born. This rhythm creates in us a longing for things to remain as they are which is inseparably tied to a certain urgency to make ready for what lies ahead. In other words, the fall calls us to enter a sea-

son of reflection and action.

Our children climb aboard big yellow buses and go back to school. In quiet moments, we may think about what it means to be parents. What are we doing? What might we do differently? Maybe we find ourselves thinking about our own childhoods. We remember the joys, as well as the more difficult times. In the garden we sit planting bulbs for spring. It is fall now, but it will be spring again and up through the earth the flowers will push toward the light, toward the sun. In the fading light of autumn, our children discover strengths as they press forward in their various athletic pursuits. We hear them calling to one another in the clear fall air. Perhaps we see in them ourselves as we once were, years ago.

The reverie of gold finally does send the message that it is time to go forward – time to do the things that have not yet been done. God gives us each a life to lead. In so many ways, God shows us what we need to do to get on with the fullness of our lives. In the fall, the Creator provides a season that stirs within us a certain urgency to go ahead with our lives push into new territory, deepen friendships, weave stronger bonds of community, take on new challenges, and become people walking toward our destinies. Fall is here.

Cheese Steak

I was driving south on Front Street in Philadelphia, taking the "scenic" route to the airport. On my left was the Delaware River, a big dark slow-moving slab of water headed for the ocean. Poking out into the water were huge docks that looked like they had last been used during World War II days. In fact, there were even a few ships tied up at these docks that appeared to be of that same vintage.

On my right, tiny streets emptied out of South Philly like narrow canals lined with block after block after block of small low-rise homes and apartments. I felt strangely comfortable as I cruised down Front Street. There were no big traffic jams, no

Manhattan style gridlock – just folks going about their business. No fast lane here in south Philadelphia.

Coming up fast was a sign that grabbed my eyes and my stomach – CHEESE STEAK – one of Philadelphia's claims to fame. A right turn signal and a quick, sliding move led me into a small parking lot – a pawnshop, a Wawa convenience store and a place with a sign that said without any pretense at all – CHEESE STEAK. I jumped out of my rented Chevy Impala and walked into the Wawa store to pick up a newspaper. I was also looking for Tums for the tummy in case the cheese steak was a little too much for me. As it turned out, the Tums were behind a locked display case along with any other substance that might even be remotely considered medicine. That's an interesting approach, I thought, to drug problems in the community.

New York Times now in hand, I somewhat cautiously opened the door into the establishment called CHEESE STEAK. It was a rather large room, neat and clean, with a huge menu on the wall above the grills and ovens. The CHEESE STEAK offered lots more than cheese steaks – all kinds of pizza and calzone, hoagies, grinders (East Coast heated sub) and of course cheese steaks with a variety of optional toppings. It was 1:30 in the afternoon and the place wasn't terribly busy.

I approached the three men behind the counter. One of the fellows looked like he might be from India, and the other two had faces that were distinctly Middle Eastern. I guessed Lebanese and the two guys were impressed with my correct guess. As it turned out, the third fellow was also Lebanese and they were brothers. The oldest of them could have passed for a young John Belushi. Believe me, it wasn't easy getting this much information from these men. Their English wasn't much better than my Lebanese, if you know what I mean. Finally, we cut to the chase and I ordered my cheese steak. There I was leaning on the counter of a place named CHEESE STEAK run by three Lebanese brothers in south Philadelphia. I watched carefully as the thin strips of steak were thrown down on the grill along with a fistful of onions. Later came the cheese placed over the mass of meat and onions, and then the whole gooey mess was spread into a soft-on-the-inside hoagie bun. Yum, yum, "deelicious." All washed down with a fountain Coke. It was gustatory glory for sure.

After my cheese steak had been reduced to bits and pieces to toy with, I soaked up the scene. A couple of well-dressed "fortyish" professional women were engaged in a conversation that led me to believe that they might be social workers. Two beefy young lads with shaved heads sat across from each other like tethered pit bulls and gorged themselves on pizza. Several young black men entered CHEESE STEAK. All three had black silky looking head rags tied tightly to their scalps. They were laughing and joking. The Lebanese owners were poker faced, and reluctant to make up a type of pizza that wasn't on the menu. Tense hip hop street talk mixed with Lebanese broken English for what seemed a tad too long a time, until finally a compromise was reached. There were smiles all around. It must have been a win-win situation.

In the far corner of the dining room, a television blared the Rikki Lake show . . . Theatre of the absurd served up at the CHEESE STEAK. The two shaved heads seemed to be paying attention to Ms. Lake's antics, but most patrons were too busy enjoying good old-fashioned Lebanese/Italian/South Philly cuisine. I played with the remnants of my meal, not really wanting to leave the CHEESE STEAK but too full to order anything else. I found myself thinking about their neighborhood. Did the residents of this area cross the bridge into New Jersey very often? Did they ever drive down to the ocean some sixty miles away? Was the area around the CHEESE STEAK mostly Catholic or Baptist or African Methodist Episcopal? How many Muslims called this little section of Philadelphia home? Whatever those answers, I knew for sure that the CHEESE STEAK and its immediate environs carried a strong sense of place, of home, of connection between people and their neighborhood.

A long way from home, I could nevertheless feel a sense of home in this urban cranny. It was good. It's where all good things human come from – a sense of connection, of roots, of place. Without these ties that bind, we're like lost souls wandering in a hopelessly empty desert. With these ties, the world is good, savory, and not lacking in possibility.

Continuing Education

Rev. William Stewart had just gotten back to Pittsburgh after his annual continuing education week at the Seminary in Richmond. He was at his desk in the Pastor's Study of Second Presbyterian Church of McKees Rocks. It was a hot, steamy August morning, the fan in the window blew the air around a bit. The whir of the fan seemed to blend with the whir in Bill's head. Upon returning from his continuing education week in Richmond, Bill often found himself swimming in a mist of half-rejuvenated theological and ecclesiastical idealism mixed in with a vague wondering about how the twists and turns of God's plan had brought him to this time and place in his life. In the quiet of the Pastor's Study, Bill thought about his wife Elizabeth. He thought about their sturdy love for each other and for their three daughters. It occurred to Bill that he and Elizabeth had now lived for twelve years in the two story parsonage next to the church at the corner of Forbes and Second Avenue. Bill remembered the day they arrived and moved in. It was just Bill, Elizabeth and Arthell the wonderdog then. There was excitement in pastoring his first church; but he had been apprehensive about living in such an urban setting, what with his roots and all his growing up years in the mountains off to the west of Virginia's Shenandoah Valley. But things had worked out. He and Elizabeth discovered the beautiful rolling country to the east of the city. They had learned to appreciate and savor the sandwiches at Primantis where they put the french fries and cole slaw right on the sandwich itself. They had even come to love those Sunday afternoon autumn warriors clad in black and gold almost as much as those native born to the city of three rivers.

This mist of memory, anticipation, longing and hope streamed through Bill's mind and heart in varying degrees of thickness that first week back from continuing education, just like it did every August. Bill found himself thinking about some of the lectures he had just recently listened to at Seminary. It occurred to him that lots of what he had heard was exciting at the time he was hearing it. Then, when he thought about it later and compared it to his own experience in the parish, well, it just lost its glow. He remembered a presentation by a young visiting professor who argued persuasively that the whole structure and mission of the Christian church had to be completely revamped if the church were going to survive into the next century. Professor LaCoursiere had all manner of sociological and cultural data in all the right places of his cerebral cortex. He was a walking information bank with up to date floppy disks firing away in his cranial cavity. Professor LaCoursiere was just "cutting edge". He urged the pastors in attendance to go back to their churches and do the revolutionary work of administering needs assessment surveys, developing support groups for every ill that can befall a parishioner, devising marketing strategies that will make the church more appealing, and, if necessary, taking the step of hiring an advertising consultant to ensure heightened visibility for the church.

Back home in McKees Rocks, Bill's mind drifted to the time when the bathroom wall in the parsonage caved in for no apparent reason. The next day, Bill called Marlin McGee, the head of the property committee, and told him what happened. The following morning Marlin arrived at the parsonage with a crew of four that included Tony Scarpatti, Bud Hargrove, Red McAllister and Yonk Matuzak. The five of them worked straight for twelve hours re-doing the bathroom wall. They got so carried away that Marlin thought the whole bathroom ought to be re-done. Appropriate expenditures were approved at the next Session meeting the following week. When all the work was completed, one Sunday, Marlin stood up and announced a grand opening of the new parsonage bathroom. Most of the congregation trooped over after church to admire the new facilities. Over coffee and cookies everyone agreed that the guys had done an outstanding job.

The Sunday after he returned from Richmond, Bill Stewart walked into the sanctuary a little bit earlier in the prelude than was his usual practice. Myrtle Simpson, the church organist, didn't blink an eye or miss a note and stayed right with the medley of old favorites, which she had put together during the week. Bill settled himself in the chair behind the pulpit. In the front pew he noticed Al and Tina Phillips and their young son Clayton. A number of years back Tina's father Joe had called Bill, and desperately explained that Tina had run off to West Virginia to live with a bunch of hippies in the mountains. He and Tina's mother, Nora, were just beside themselves and wanted Bill to drive down to Mossy Glade and see if he could talk some sense into Tina's head. A couple of days later, Bill was on a mission to Mossy Glade. After hours of curving highways south of Pittsburgh, Bill found himself sitting at a table with a group of folks who looked like a cross between a bunch of 2nd century Celtic warriors and devotees of a Hindu guru. It was all very peaceful as they shared a casserole of brown rice, natural peanut butter and organic cucumbers, washed down with large swigs of honey-sweetened kumquat juice. After the meal, 17-year-old Tina showed Bill around the "community", and explained why she and her friends had chosen to "drop out" and live this new life. Bill told Tina what had been going on in McKees Rocks, and that her parents missed her and were terribly worried about her. Tina wound up missing her whole junior year of high school. The following August she came back to McKees Rocks, made up the missed year in night school and graduated with her class. Later on she met Al at Robert Morris College. Bill Stewart thought about all of this during Myrtle's prelude. He also thought about Clayton's baptism. He remembered a damp late spring Sunday morning when he had held little Clayton at the front of the church, and pronounced the words, "Clayton Weatherby Phillips, I baptize you in the name of the Father and of the Son and of the Holy Spirit. Amen." Al and Tina beamed their happiness throughout the sanctuary. Joe and Nora wiped tears of joy from the corners of their eyes.

Myrtle had finished up her old favorites medley and the church had been disquietingly quiet for almost two minutes before Bill Stewart came out of his reverie, stood up, and welcomed people to worship. The choir did a stirring rendition of *Blessed Assurance*, and Bill thought to himself that he was glad to be back at Second Presbyterian of McKees Rocks. A young family no one knew visited the church that morning. That coming week Bill was going to talk with someone from the county about what might be involved in developing a Senior Meals site at the church. The Men's Club would be meeting on Thursday to make preliminary plans for the annual deer hunting trip up to Pop McGill's camp in Potter County. It was August. Soon the heat would begin to fade and fall would be in the air. Sunday School would start up again. Renewed energy would fuel new projects at Second Presbyterian of McKees Rocks. That night the Braves beat the Pirates with a ninth inning home run. The game was a little disappointing, but that night Rev. Bill Stewart gave thanks to God from the bottom of his heart for bringing him to McKees Rocks, and giving him the opportunity to learn about the straightforward, honest beauty of life together in covenant with God and with each other. Bill slept well.

Monday morning was a little cooler than the week before. Bill didn't turn on the fan in the Pastor's Study. The mist of reflection had given way to the clarity of direct perception. On Bill's desk was a note from the Church Secretary, Lillian Thompson. It read, "Please call Yonk Matuzak first thing when you come in. He wants to talk with you about getting the Christian Education wing ready for the fall."

Yonk's Amazing Christmas

It was mid-December and a cold wind was tearing down from Lake Erie, whipping the Ohio River into a froth and whistling around the windows of Yonk's house at the corner of Center Avenue and Bellvue Street in the North Boroughs of Pittsburgh, Pennsylvania. Yonk had taken over the front bedroom that looked out over the river. Yonk figured that when his wife of 40 years, Estelle, began raising a fuss about how loudly he snored, she probably had her eyes on the front bedroom. Yonk drew the line and cut a deal with Estelle. If she wanted her own Yonk-less, snore-free bedroom, then he would fix up daughter Wanda's old bedroom and Estelle could have that one with it's picturesque view of Leon's Auto Body and Repair Shop. Yonk was not about to give up the front bedroom. He could not imagine not being able to sit in that dark upstairs room smoking a Have-a-Tampa cigar and looking out the window over Ohio River Boulevard and Neville Island to the just barely visible River Road Inn, home of the best turtle soup in all of western Pennsylvania.

As the cold wind blew around the eaves, Yonk was asleep in the bedroom he had fought to hold on to. He was dreaming, only of course he didn't know he was dreaming. It was all so real. He was dreaming that Terry Bradshaw was still the Steelers' quarterback. The crowd was on its feet screaming joyfully into the cold, gray December sky. Bradshaw had just thrown another touchdown pass, and the Steelers were in the process of blowing out Bum Philips and the rest of the bums from Houston.

Just about the time Bradshaw had arrived back on the side-lines, Yonk woke up to the ugly reality that he had been dreaming again. The phone was ringing. Yonk's heart jumped a beat when the voice on the other end of the line announced that she was calling from the Emergency Room at Allegheny General Hospital. The voice on the other end of the line explained that Maxine McSwain had been brought into the hospital with what appeared to be a heart attack. Yonk's abrupt transition to waking consciousness resulted in a loud scream, "Estelle, it's the hospital, your mother's there with a heart attack!"

There followed a hub-bub in Yonk's and Estelle's home that ranked right up there with the time the news came about Davey Boy Green taking his rifle into the empty church building and shooting the place up one Wednesday afternoon. There was yelling and swearing and slamming doors and loud questions aimed at God above. Estelle began to weep loudly when Yonk insisted on heating up some water so he could have a cup of java for the drive to the hospital.

When they finally got to Allegheny General, Maxine wasn't doing very well. There was lots of scrambling around by doctors and nurses and others. Estelle was up next to her 88-year-old mother, clutching on to her arm and stroking her forehead lightly – Yonk figured it must be bad if the doctors were letting Estelle hang all over Maxine that way. Yonk excused himself from the bedside scene and went back out to the waiting room. He sat down and began to glance mindlessly at the sports section of the Pittsburgh Press – "Stoudt-led Steelers crushed by Cleveland" – Yonk thought to himself, "Cliff Stoudt, what a joke, if only Bradshaw was still around."

It was 3:00 a.m. and Yonk was sitting in the waiting room at Allegheny General. Not much more than fifty feet away, his mother-in-law Maxine McSwain was probably dying as his wife Estelle looked on. Yonk thought about Maxine, whom he had known for over 40 years. They'd had their ups and downs over the years. Yonk had always thought Maxine was a bit snooty and pushy. He remembered how, when he and Estelle first got married, Maxine was always telling Yonk that he should take Estelle down to the Jersey shore for a summer vacation. Yonk never could understand why anybody would drive all the way to the ocean when Lake Erie was just a couple of hours to the north.

Maxine was still alive and actually starting to rally by the time Yonk left to go back home to get ready for the 7:00 a.m. shift at the soap factory on Neville Island. Estelle wasn't crying anymore, and the hospital people weren't scrambling all about as they had been before. It looked to Yonk as though Maxine was going to pull through it this time. "She's sure a tough old bird," he thought to himself.

Over the next week to ten days, Maxine continued to improve. Every day after Yonk left for work, Estelle would get on the 17b Avalon bus and go down to Manchester and then walk over to the hospital. After work, Yonk would stop at home, check the mail and then head on down to the hospital. The days till Christmas began to dwindle. On the evening of the 23rd, Yonk did his usual after work routine. When he arrived at Maxine's room, he found almost all her children and grandchildren there. There was lots of loud talking and laughing. Yonk stood in the doorway and looked at the little "rug rats" as he called them.

They were having the time of their little lives, just crawling around, pushing one another in the wheelchair, jumping up on Grandma's bed, begging her for just one more piece of candy. Estelle was sitting at a table right in front of a south facing window. Yonk could see Three Rivers Stadium in the distance. She was playing Chinese checkers with her little niece Elfreida. It was quite a scene there, all those little "knee biters" with their mothers and fathers and Maxine lying there with a big smile on her face and now just one or two tubes sticking into her. Yonk felt something kind of give way inside of him and the next thing he knew he had some tears rolling down his cheeks. Estelle looked up right at that very moment and her blue eyes caught Yonk straight on. She smiled the way she hadn't for a long time.

On the way home that night, Yonk and Estelle stopped at the River Road Inn. They both had the turtle soup. Over his second bowl, Yonk explained to Estelle that he really thought Maxine shouldn't live by herself anymore. He'd been thinking . . . . he had saved about 5,000 dollars to do some work on his deer camp up in Potter County. Yonk figured that the deer camp was OK as it was. He looked right at Estelle and said, "I want to use that money to fix up Thelma's old bedroom at home. That way Maxine'll be right down the hall from us in case anything like this ever happens again. That's just what I want to do."

Estelle smiled back across the table. Yonk looked down at his 10 dollar Casio digital watch. It was past midnight. It was Christmas Eve and he had to be at work at 7:00 a.m. They headed back home and by 12:30 Yonk was asleep, dreaming again.

More Power to You

Somehow I felt it before I woke up. Something had happened in the night. As the sleep cleared from my brain, I heard the rain falling on the roof. The moisture in the air was not falling as snow, but rather as rain. The tapping on the roof was familiar and comforting as was the view from the bedroom window – big puddles of water on the street with a steady rain still falling. The earth was dark and wet and filled with the promise of summer's green. The morning made me feel two different ways – I wanted to rise quickly, get dressed, and be out in the rain, sniffing the scent of a new season. But I also wanted to stretch deeply, and roll right back into the comfort of cool sheets and a light blanket. I wondered if bears feel this kind of ambivalence when first coming out of the den. I like thinking of myself as just another one of God's critters who is as much a part of natural cycles as the wolf, the deer, the river and the spruce bog.

When I first read the great naturalist, John Muir's accounts of his woodland romps, I thought this fellow sounded a tad off the level. In one piece, Muir described being out in the High Sierras during a howling January blizzard. Somehow traipsing along the earth was not enough for this wild Scot. He wanted to get up off the ground to feel the full fury of the storm. So Muir found a large sturdy pine and climbed way up into its lofty branches where he hung on for dear life as the wind drove the snow deep into the recesses of his bushy beard. I wondered if this great naturalist was something more of a troubled soul with a death wish. All I could picture was hypothermia setting in. But after hours up in his windy, snowy aerie

Muir came sliding down that big pine with a shine on his face as if he had just met his Maker face to face.

Years later now, I don't think Muir really was wacky at all. Rather, I think he was more willing to act on impulses that many of us have felt but have, for the most part, shied away from actually acting on. Some of us worry what other people might think if they saw us climbing a big white pine in our backyard. Others of us might question our own sanity, even as we prepared to run from the sauna over the lake to punch through the hole in the ice. And what might the neighbors say if you and your bride of 40 years were seen making snow angles in the backyard?

I say, "Relax, don't worry about what they think or say." Despite all the works of civilization that have lifted us out of the realm of pure nature, we are nevertheless creatures with a memory for the ancient, and the eternal. We feel in our blood that we are yet interwoven with the natural world. When you hear the call of the wild, I say howl back. When you hear the call of the wild, I say it's our Creator reminding us that we are not self-created. We are of a deeper stream that flows from timeless springs seeping from beneath the gates of Eden. So when you feel that Muir-like urge to be baptized in the joy of God's world, I say, "More power to you!"

Visions from New Jersey

It's late October and I'm sitting in a Starbucks coffee shop in Medford, New Jersey. Medford is a cutesy little town, about 25 miles east of Philadelphia, that has managed to preserve its downtown colonial buildings, but around the edges it is full blown Jersey suburbia. I have just consumed a small caramel frappuccino®, and I'm actually feeling a little ill. That sweet frozen concoction tasted great while it was going down the hatch, but now I'm feeling bloated by it's heaviness and sweetness.

Several groups of high school age youth come and then go, having satisfied their craving for caffeine and sugar. Over the cleverly concealed stereo speakers I hear the voice of Canadian singer/songwriter Gordon Lightfoot. The melody is pure and the words create a picture of a wild northern frontier, where nature still calls the shots. Hearing this song in a suburban Starbucks is more than a tad ironic. About ten feet away to my left is a table surrounded by four young females. I guess that they are probably seniors in high school, but their makeup and understated chic clothes creates the appearance of young women in their mid to late twenties. They talk quietly with that edge of sophisticated detachment that suggests that they may well be members of the "ruling caste" at their local high school. Other people come and go through the doors of this caffeine paradise. There are some young mothers with their little ones all decked out in L.L. Bean trail wear. A couple of skinny middle-aged fellows come through the doors. They're dressed up in running tights and fancy Gore-tex jackets. (I remember when people wore sweats to go running.) From the looks of it, a safe bet in this "bear market" would be to invest in products that contain caffeine and sugar. (Pastoral disclaimer: I am not *really* suggesting that anyone *really* go out and do this, however.)

Outside Starbucks' big glass window is a parking lot, and lots and lots of stores, arranged in such a way that you're encouraged to create the fiction that you're not really at a mall. But the truth is, you are. Maple trees have been planted in every nook and cranny of available soil. Most of these trees look to be in the neighborhood of thirty to forty years old. The maples really are quite pretty; most of them have turned the bright oranges and reds of peak autumn.

"Pst, pst, hey hon, you looking at the trees? You like the fall colors, huh? I like'm too. Hey hon, you want me to read your palm?" The voice came from over my right shoulder. I turned and met the gaze of a women with long, dark, flowing hair framing a slightly oval face. Her eyes were hazel, but of a brighter and greener shade than I'd ever seen before. Around her neck was a heavy silver necklace adorned with greenish stones that were a pretty good match for her eyes. She was wearing what appeared to be a very simple one-piece dress made out of a rough, earthy fabric with shades of brown and straw colors. She was not only pretty; she was exotic, as if she had just strayed away from a caravan bound for some remote valley in central Asia. I stared at her, kind of dumbfounded by the whole situation.

"You alright?" she said. "I just wanted to know if you wanted to have your palm read. That's what I do. . . . mostly a little palm reading, some psychic stuff as well. But it looks like you're more interested in the trees, which is fine because, you know, I really like the trees too. I really like the trees at this time of year, because to me it's like the trees are laughing because they love the color of their leaves; but they're also crying because they know winter is coming and soon the leaves will be blown in all four directions. Did you ever hear the trees laughing and crying? I bet you they're laughing today. You want to go outside and see if we can hear the trees laughing?"

So, I'm following this lady into the parking lot and I'm thinking, this is nuts. A stray fragment of a thought creeps across my brain. I think, "That dress is so baggy she could have one huge knife hidden or maybe even a gun. Well, it's too late now because she's already got her ear pressed up against a young maple and she's calling me over to share in the "conversation." "Can you hear what this one's saying? Come closer," she says.

I put my ear right up next to the tree trunk. I hear nothing but the traffic from the nearby highway. I shake my head. She says, "Be still and listen." I try again and still only get the sounds of Highway 61. And then she says, "You're trying too hard. You're trying too hard. Just relax and let the voices come to you."

It was something about the phrase – *let the voices come to you* – that stirred me to step back from the tree and reach out to shake hands with this Jersey gypsy, and let her know that it had been a pleasure to meet her, but it was time for me to jump in my Hertz rent-a-car and head on down the line. As we shook hands she tried to get a look at my palm. I resisted and she said, "Well at least get yourself some lotion. Your hands are dry as the desert."

"God be with you," I said.

"And with you too," she smiled.

The next day I am crossing the Delaware River by the way of the enormous Ben Franklin Bridge. Hello, Pennsylvania. Goodbye, New Jersey. It costs three dollars to cross the bridge from east to west, and nothing if you're going the other way. Downtown Philadelphia sits off to the right at about 1:00 . . . floating like the emerald city on a sea of urban sprawl. "God is here. God is everywhere," I say to myself. God is the Mystery . . . the Creator from whom all that is proceeds. All that is remains connected to the Creator. I gradually slow down in anticipation of reaching the toll booth ahead. The sacred, shimmering light of the divine is all around us, all of the time, beckoning, leading, enlightening.

All Is Well

High up on a spur of the Laurentian Divide, it was getting late. To the west, the sky was filled with layers of red-orange clouds, a display that seems to appear more often at this time of year than at any other. I don't know what creates these late fall tongues of fire, but I strongly associate them with the final transition from fall to winter. I could look that sky fire for hours, but there isn't time. It's getting dark. And actually the clouds burn their brightest for just a brief while anyway.

Before I fall asleep that night, I'm granted the gift of seeing the fire clouds one more time. The viewing is in my mind's eye this time, but the colors and lines and contrasts are sharp and beautiful. I find myself thinking of various people who have come and gone in my life. I'm thinking of people in our church who have left this mortal life and now live eternally with God. A kind of quiet darkness descends around me, but it's not a heavy thick darkness. Rather, it's a depth of darkness surrounded at the edges by a penumbra of light that eases the sense of aloneness. It's comforting.

A week or so later, I can't remember just when, I'm heading down the hill from Eveleth on Highway 53 to Virginia. It's getting toward sunset, and the clouds are thickening up on the west. I don't know what triggered the first tear, but I think it had something to do with a member of our church family being seriously ill. That made me think about all the people whose funerals I've been involved in over the years. And at that moment I'm flooded with very clear pictures of these people. Their spirits are just drifting peacefully up out of the bowl in which Virginia is located. This is not the least bit morbid. It's peaceful. And I'm remembering these people through their stories and my association with them. And that is good.

The tears that are dripping down my face are the tears of joy – joy at having walked the road with these people; joy in knowing that somehow in this large, beautiful universe, these souls are alright – that they are in God's keeping and the light of their souls shines brighter now than it ever did in this world of flesh and blood.

The thought crosses my mind that, on the far side of what we can rationally conceive, there is an opening out from the present into the future which, as it turns out, really is a realm of light. On cold late fall nights the citizens of that realm gather on rocky beaches and light bonfires to let their loved ones know that all is well.

The tongues of fire that we see in the western sky at this time of year are the good wishes of those we will always love. The light of their souls and the light of their bonfires are meant to assure us that for them and for us *All is well.*

Wolf-Kill

Right in front of our little farmhouse, you could see it when we drove up. It was the fairly intact hide of a whitetail deer. A few bones were scattered about, including a remarkably well-preserved foreleg. Right there in our front yard, just a few yards off the county road was an obvious wolf-kill. These ancestors of our canine pets must have been hungry when they took this deer down, because there really was not much left. I found myself wondering what this hunt must have been like . . . . . lots of questions. Did the deer run a long way before being taken down by the wolves? How large was the pack? Did the deer fall somewhere else? Was the carcass then dragged to the front of the house? Or did the deer give up its spirit (and flesh) right there in front of the farmhouse? Was it over quickly for the deer – a swift carnivorous bite to the jugular? Or was it a slow agonizing death, legs with tendons ripped, unable to move as the troop of slavering wolves tore out chunks of flesh, even as the deer's heart pumped consciousness into it's brain? Does the brain of a deer release certain chemicals that ease the passage from life to death? Lots of questions . . .

I looked at the fur and the bones, and I could not escape some of the sense of horror – one set of God's creatures tearing another to pieces so that they would have the fuel inside to make it through the rest of the winter, to feed their young, to reproduce, to create a next generation, to survive . . . pretty Darwinian. I looked skyward . . . a bright blue April day after lots of rain. The earth was still cold and bare. Only the soft gray fur of the pussy willows hinted that change was not too far away.

I picture the native people who were here for all those many years before we arrived. When they took a creature like a deer or in those early days a woodland caribou, the hunters offered a prayer to the Creator and the hunted before the final stroke or thrust that ended the animal's life. They thanked the Creator for providing the game and they thanked the animal for giving its flesh for food. It was clear that something Sacred was transpiring on these occasions. I find myself drawn to that vision of the Sacred – a moment, a place in time where the eternal dance is made manifest in something that we might otherwise consider mundane. The Ojibwe hunter recognized this connection between the Creator and the created. The moment of the kill brought forth prayer in the most natural way.

Standing under the spring sky, I am aware that the death of this deer is more than just a mess of fur and blood and flesh. The fact that I could view this scene as "carnage" reveals just how deeply modern consciousness has been "sanitized", to its own detriment. The world that our Creator made is one that is filled with a certain fierceness that can inspire us to begin seeing just how intricate, beautiful and interconnected life really is. I pray to God to save us all from those forces that would, under the guise of making the world safer, try to eliminate or cover up the blood, the flesh, the bone and the fur. These things bring us a sense of the fleeting nature of life, the preciousness of life, and the call to live life with energy and passion – like the deer and the wolf.

When all our forests have been turned into tree farms and/or parks, and our wild game is no longer wild, we will have lost something of God. We will have lost a principal means of connecting with the Divine. The wildness of God's world will be

sullied by humans who have come to associate blood with death rather than life. So great will be the fear of death for some of us that we will forget how to live.

The wolf-kill in our front yard is a sign of a deeper order that human beings are a part of whether, they are willing to acknowledge it or not. The wolf-kill is a call to wake-up to one's place in the circle of life. Ultimately, the blood and bone and fur beckon us to fulfill our own unique destinies as children of God. To deny that the human order is part of God's embrace of all creation, is to commit to a path of "hubris". The Divine always finds ways to restore harmony when "hubris" has led to chaos and disorder. This restoration of balance is not in doubt. It is only a matter of time.

On the Way to Eveleth

The air on that late October day was heavy and cold. The gray of encroaching winter reached right down to the tops of the white pines with the promise of snow. Something was in the air.

Still, when the news came it was shocking. Senator Paul Wellstone and all aboard the small plane were dead. The plane had gone down in that thick cold and gray as it approached the airport in Eveleth. They had, in the closing days of a heated election, come north to attend a funeral in Virginia. A journey of compassion and respect had instead led to death in a remote marsh in northern Minnesota. It was a part of the state that this passionate and cerebral Senator had come to love. The Mesabi Iron Range was where the Senator's fervent populism had first caught fire two terms ago. Now the land of the red earth, Mesabi Red, became the place where his spirit was given up, along with his wife's and daughter's and the others' lives aboard the ill-fated flight.

As evening fell, spiritual leaders gathered on the front steps of the capitol in St. Paul to speak to the throng of grieving Minnesotans. The drums of Native American people seemed most fitting as they pounded out a message of sadness and loss. It was easy to imagine these drumbeats waking up the spirits of the land outside Eveleth. It was easy to imagine Ojibwe voices comforting those who had so recently given up their mortal bodies for a kind of being they had only known before in their dreams. It was good to find some comfort emerge from the terrible reality of a small plane slamming into the earth in a burst of flames. . . . the horror and tragedy of lives lost.

When famous people die in the prime of their lives, we may find ourselves touched as if that person had actually been a member of our own family. It's about some link of common humanity – some spirit of empathy that recognizes and grieves the inevitability of tragedy in this mortal human life. In dwelling on the event we may find ourselves thinking about various situations where our own life brushed death; where, but for some uncontrolled factor one way or another sometimes called the Grace of God, we would have found ourselves crushed or burned out of our embodied existence. It is sobering and mysterious at the same time. For a few weeks following the Senator's death, I found myself hugging my wife and children more often. All my relationships seemed to take on a glowing sense of being cherished. I even said some things to people I'd been meaning to say but hadn't because, well, many of us are brought up to avoid too much depth of feeling, tears and the like. It was all good, though.

It might not have been Paul Wellstone, but given who he was, it was particularly appropriate that his death would also prompt questions about what one was doing with one's life. Whether you agreed with him on issues or not (my southern Democrat father once described Wellstone as one breath away from being a Socialist), you could not deny his passion and his zeal for asking important questions. As the cold gloom of October gave way to some milder days in November, I found myself periodically sliding into reveries of self-examination, questioning myself about the things I believe: Are my beliefs and my actions in sync? Am I willing to speak my truth? Do I know my truth? Am I willing to accept the consequences for speaking the truth as I see it? I suspect I was not the only Minnesotan asking myself these kinds of questions.

When the Senator and his party got on the plane that morning, they rightly assumed that they were on the way to Eveleth – that they would proceed to Virginia for the funeral and then to Duluth for a debate that evening. It didn't work out that way. On the way to Eveleth, fate led them instead into eternity. And so it is with all of us. At any point along the way, our own destination may be changed to eternity. And in the between time, the spirits of our ancestors, and the voice of the Creator, urge us to live this life fully with passion and integrity . . .

"l'chaim"

Benediction

I See Hope

It's cold. I see brick walls on Chestnut Street.
I see the mortar falling out.
I see storefronts standing empty
and others that need paint.
I see hope.

Kids stand around nearby their school,
some wrapped against the cold. Some not.
Some with letter jackets, some with army surplus,
some sport labels that exclaim superiority.
Some stand there with the blessings of home,
others carry only the burdens.
I see hope.

The newspaper tells of this group and that,
of grudges and greed and power lust,
of orchids and onions, and passion and principle.
I see hope.

All over the Range the word tolls grim.
More cutbacks, more layoffs,
more fear for the future.
Better pack the wagon and head for California,
maybe the Cities.
We're told a way of life is on the wane.
I see hope.

Suburban dreams encroach on mighty lakes
and thin sweet rivers.
Cabins give way to Taj Mahals
and highways are jammed by exurban commuters.
The cost of gas is high.
The miles per gallon are low.
I see hope.

Music on the radio comes from faraway.
It's loud. It's angry.
Or it's sweet and phony
and made by robots in a basement somewhere.
I see hope.

Old people walk the streets of their childhood.
They carry the wisdom of place in mind and soul.
Some people don't listen to them.
Some do.
I see hope.

I see people I don't know, aimless on the street.
Where they've been, where they are,
where they're going, it's all the same.
They're ragged around the edges
and their clothes shout Goodwill.
I see hope.

In the hospital I see a face I know.
He's fighting hard to keep his life.
Surrounded by plastic and glass,
punctured by needles and tubes.
A wan smile crosses his lips,
the slightest twinkle in his eyes.
I see hope.

It's cold, almost 25° below.
The red dawn carries the promise of snow.
A Monson truck turns north on 53.
A long day to Dryden and back.
I see hope.

Darkness wraps us on a late winter night.
New lamps bring light downtown.
Old lights burn with memory.
A small man and a large dog
meditate beneath the towering maples.
Its branches quiver and breathe
and stretch out to receive the falling snow.
I see hope.

New and Recent Releases from
Singing River Publications, Inc.

Perspectives Through Black Ice, by Christine Moroni
   Reflections on the seasons of the year — seasons of the human heart — designed to be read in the early morning light of sunrise or by the glow of evening twilight.

Cow Pies & Bases, by Robert B. Coates
   Warm, funny, poignant and engaging, this book offers an honest, unabashed account of growing up in rural mid-America just after World War II.

Let Your Light Shine, by Ann King Lishinski
   A richly illustrated book for children of all ages to remind us that anything is possible if we try, and that we live on in ways we never could have foreseen.

Jordan's Near Side, by Frank Stafford Davis
   Windows into how the Sacred manifests in nature and in the ordinariness of our daily lives, drawn from the author's experience as a parish pastor on Minnesota's Mesabi Iron Range.

Available through:
   Singing River Publications, Inc.
   P.O. Box 72
   Ely, MN 55731
   www.speravi.com/singingriver

About the Author

Frank Stafford Davis was born and raised in Atlanta, Georgia. He was ordained to ministry in the Presbyterian Church U.S.A. in 1982, and currently serves as a parish pastor on Minnesota's Mesabi Iron Range. He holds advanced degrees from Yale Divinity School (Master of Divinity) and Duquesne University (Master and Ph.D. in Psychology), and has previously worked as a boarding school chaplain and an outpatient psychotherapist. Frank is a 1974 graduate of Williams College, Williamstown, Massachusetts, where he majored in Religion.

Frank made the photographs on the cover and on pages viii, 4, 6, 13, 14, 52, 53, 54, 56, 58, 60, 64, 68, 77, 79, 81, 88, and 92.

About the Photographer

Peter Martin was born in St. Paul, Minnesota, and raised in Britt, Minnesota. He holds a Bachelor of Fine Arts degree from Minneapolis College of Art and Design. Peter also earned an M.A. in Journalism from the University of Minnesota. He is an adjunct faculty member at the University of Minnesota's School of Journalism and Mass Communication as well as the School of Design, Housing and Apparel.
He can be contacted by e-mail at Pete@PixelPete.com

Peter made the photographs on pages 10, 11, 17, 22, 24, 28, 30, 33, 36, 45, 47, 49, 73, 85, 87, 90, and 94.

Peter also did the production work associated with the digitization of all photographs, including those on pages 20 and 38.